365 Limericks You Won't Find Anywhere Else

A Humorous Collection for All Ages

RON RICH

365 Limericks You Won't Find Anywhere Else:
A Humorous Collection for All Ages

Published by 40 String Press
Lakewood, CO

ronrichauthor.com

ISBN: 979-8-234-03488-5

HUMOR / Form / Limericks & Verse

Cover design by Amanda Miller.
Layout design by Bryan Canter.

In memory
of my wife, Joyce

GIVE ME THE WORDS

Give me the words I need, to read, and write, and learn;
We'll find them in books, on every page we turn.
Give me the words that sing out in rhyme;
I'll say "Read it again," time after time.

Give me the words and letters that say the alphabet;
I'll name people and places, and things I haven't
even seen yet.
Give me the words and numbers for counting
this and that;
Things that can be long or short, or tall or flat.

Give me the words that tell me how and why;
I'll have answers about our earth, and sea, and sky.
Give me the words I need, to become a reader;
I'll grow and learn, to become a leader.

Give me the words that can only be found in a book;
I'll find more to make me think, with each new look.
Give me the words I need, to be happy and wise;
We'll find them together, in the books we prize.

THE LIMERICKS

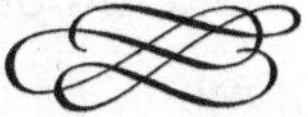

I have a friend named Jimmy Glen
Who likes working out at the gym.
He goes every day
Without a delay.
Not like me, who goes now and then.

There was a cook in Philadelphia
Named Anna Maria Olivia.
There was only one dish
She knew how to fix.
Italian Vegetarian Lasagnia.

There was a young man named Harry
Who went daily to the library.
He only read one book
Which made others look.
Was that really necessary?

There was a man who ate only soup;
Never vegetables or fruit.
He really didn't care
If it was thin or thicker
As long as it tasted like soup.

There was a skater named Patty Price
Who fell seven times on the ice.
She quickly jumped up,
Bruises on her butt.
And no broken bones, that is nice!

There was a lad who lived in Prague,
Who owned a little three-legged dog.
It could not run fast;
Lost a leg in the past
Jumping out of a truck in a fog.

There was a young lady in Kuwait
Who was never on time, always late.
On her final day
Someone had to say
"She'll be late at the Pearly Gate."

A preacher in Kalamazoo
Said, "Love many, hate few."
People heard his words—
We're not all lovebirds
But we'll certainly do it for you.

There was a mother in Hilton Head
Who said, "Please, always make your bed."
Her children listened well
As far as I can tell
But they didn't do what she said.

There was a man named Billy Barnett
Who said we should "forgive and forget."
Forgiving is not easy;
Forgetting makes us queasy.
Billy's idea is the best!

There was a teacher in Lover's Grove
Who said, "Keep your eye on the road."
That's pretty good advice.
You should listen twice
To your driving instructor, I'm told.

A man stopped reading his novel
When asked to pee in a bottle.
There was a crack in it
And before he quit
The puddle he made was awful.

My doctor had that look in her eye;
Made me think she might be a spy.
Finding spots on my skin
And glad to freeze them;
She said, "That's it for a year." Goodbye.

There was a gentleman named Price
Who said, "I'll never get tired of life."
I've got friends galore,
Enemies by the score
And they all give me lots of advice."

I know a man called Willy Witt
And when he says "no," he means it.
He doesn't consider workers;
He thinks they are shirkers
And they all say they would like to quit.

There was a lady in Leavenworth
Who always sang too loud in church.
Morning or afternoon,
She sang out of tune,
Which made the saints want to curse.

There was a lady in Brussels
Who liked to do jigsaw puzzles.
She worked day and night
To get it just right
And a lost piece always meant trouble.

There was a young man in Dunkirk
Who once had a flat tire at work.
Nobody helped him
Or gave him a grin
Because they all thought he was a jerk.

The wife of a well-known preacher
Was a favorite Sunday School teacher.
She knew her lessons
for every session
But she was a long-winded reader.

A handsome young man from Boone's Lick
Liked to teach his little dog tricks.
He gave him a treat
For each little feat
But the dog wouldn't even chase sticks.

There was an old man in Nantucket
Who kept candy in a bucket.
He ate one every day
Which caused him to say:
"I savor the taste of each nugget."

There was a man from the Old Country
Who had a large sum of money.
He put it in a bank
Located in Fairbanks
Until he spent it on his honey.

A large lady sang in the opera
And that's where she sang an aria.
Everything was fine,
Nothing out of line.
Then she fell and broke her tibia.

There was a young man from Sumatra
Who really liked to eat pasta.
He ate it every day,
Fixed in so many ways,
But he liked it best with ricotta.

There was a young man in Berlin
Who did not have a pot to pee in.
He was very poor,
But that was before
His lottery ticket was cashed in.

I saw a young man on the turnpike
Who rode to work one day on his bike.
It had just three wheels,
Which was quite ideal.
This was not a bike but a trike.

There was a very strange old man
Who liked to smash soda-pop cans.
He had quite a few,
A thousand or two
Which he kept in his minivan.

A smart young lady named Gertie
Did her Christmas shopping early.
She bought so much stuff
She had more than enough.
Where to put it all made her worry.

There was a mailman named Malachi
Who looked people right in the eye.
It made some nervous;
One said, “What’s the purpose?”
When asked why, he would not reply.

There was a soul named Ken Kramer
Who was always kind to strangers.
Rich or poor, no matter,
Some thin and some fatter.
He never thought of them as dangers.

There was a cop named Terry Westin
Who was always asking questions.
He recorded answers
And ignored stammers
As he took every confession.

There was a mother named Wanda Wright
Who read to her children every night.
What book to choose;
One they will approve.
She never failed to satisfy.

A young man known as a Quaker
Was always nice to his neighbors.
Difficult or easy,
Careful but speedy.
He did all this without favors.

There was an old man in Santa Fe
Who told everyone, “Have a nice day.”
He tried to talk more,
And people implored,
But surprise, that is all he would say.

There was a boy in the Florida Keys
Who always remembered to say “please.”
No one understood him
And he made their heads spin
Because he said it in Portuguese.

A worker named Willy B. Bright
Said "The customer is always right."
One started a riot.
No one was quiet.
And Willy left on the next flight.

Met a lad at the Holiday Inn
Who didn't know how to swim.
Afraid of the pool, he felt like a fool.
So now, he plays the violin.

There was a young man named Bailey Beale
Who always ate well-balanced meals.
His diet was strict.
He made it all click
So he could have muscles of steel.

There was a worker at Pizza Hut
Who did the right thing, no matter what.
He always tried hard
And he stayed on guard.
For him, there could be no screw-up.

There was a man from Trinidad
Who counted to ten when he got mad.
He tried this every time
And that was always fine
Because he was a good soccer dad.

There was a waitress named Karen Klink
Who had more patience than you might think.
Bad things could happen,
Causing distractions.
She always had a smile and a wink.

There was a young man, worked at Starbucks
And he always kept his mouth shut.
He forgot one day
When he had something to say
And everyone there suddenly hushed.

There was a young man named Sam Pete
Who always kept his desk quite neat.
He stayed overtime,
Once in a while 'til nine,
Which certainly kept him off the street.

There was an old man named Max
Who talked about people behind their backs.
Sometimes he told lies
Which made people cry.
And those are the hard, cold facts.

There was a girl named Ronda Rohr
Who always left her shoes at the door.
A dog chewed them up.
And that was bad luck!
"I won't leave them there anymore."

There was a young man from Guam
Who began each day with a song.
Sometimes too loud
Which brought a crowd.
And he asked them to sing along.

There was a girl from Battle Creek
Who read the dictionary all week.
Want a definition?
That was her mission!
Everyone thought she was unique.

There was a lady from Santa Cruz
Who was wearing uncomfortable shoes.
Two sizes too small,
Every day, I recall.
And some might call that self-abuse.

There was a man from another state
Who could never admit his mistakes.
He made a correction;
Got a new direction.
He had a lot fewer headaches.

There was a young husband named Skipper
Who always spoke in a whisper.
Caused by a big fight
With his unhappy wife,
She hit his head with a glass pitcher.

There was a young boy named Bryce
Who wanted to see the sunrise.
He could not stay awake
Until the daybreak
No matter how many times he tried.

There was a young man named Paul Polk
Who would not write a thank you note.
He knew he should.
He knew he could.
And some of his friends called him a dope!

There was a boy named Alexander
Who didn't have very good manners.
He wouldn't say please
Which should be a breeze.
When asked why—he had no answers!

A man who worked for *The New York Times*
Would not obey the speed-limit signs.
When he got stopped
By a New York cop
He knew he had committed a crime!

There was a lady named Lorraine
Who was always the one to complain.
She could spoil a party,
Never say sorry
And she gave everyone a migraine!

A certain store on a street named Quail
Had a going-out-of-business sale.
The prices were low
As far as I know.
They didn't miss a single detail.

A talkative fellow named Roy Rice
Was always giving people advice.
Talked about anything,
Wiser than you think.
He had advice for all but his wife.

There was a man named Danny Dirk
And he was never on time for work.
He often missed roll-call,
No surprise at all.
Soon, he was no longer a file clerk.

There was an old man from Oregon
Who would not apologize when wrong.
He knew he should;
An unlikelihood.
His wife said he was a moron.

There was a weird man named Cecil
Who laughed and made fun of people.
He had a few friends
And made no amends.
He was strange and sometimes evil.

There was a mother named Linda Lynn
Who gave birth to a set of twins.
She may need standbys,
What a big surprise!
A year later, she did it again!

A cook in the month of October
Let a very large pot boil over.
What a great big mess!
He was quite perplexed!
Now he will cook a lot slower.

There was a lady named Susie Clouse
Who would not leave her beautiful house.
She kept the doors shut,
And she would not get up;
Not even for cookies from the Scouts!

There was a lady from New Jersey
Who was always one to worry.
She ignored common sense,
Had no self-confidence,
And her whole world was topsy-turvy!

There was a girl from Angel Fire
Who said she was always quite tired.
Fell asleep on the job
And then began to sob.
Now you know, that's why she got fired.

There was a young girl named Abbey
Who was always very happy.
And then one day she fell,
And she began to yell,
"I think that I bruised my knee-cappy!"

There was a young lady from Riding
Who seemed to be always crying.
She just could not stop,
Even for her friend Scott.
The whole thing was most terrifying!

There was a young man from Old Fort Wayne
Who wanted to fly a big plane.
He could not pass the test
And that was for the best,
Because he was quite a scatterbrain.

There was a young man named Enrique
Who met a stranger in the street.
Who can he be?
Will he like me?
Is this someone to save or delete?

There was a young boy named Sloan
Who, one day, ran away from home.
He was only ten;
He won't do it again.
He did not like being alone.

There was a young lass named Millie
Who wanted to live in Chile.
When I asked her why,
She replied, "Oh my,"
"That's where I met my friend Willie!"

There was a girl from Butternut
Who never did not like to wake up.
She slept until noon
And missed her homeroom.
And now, her grades really do suck.

There was a man from Beaver Creek
Who slept for a day and a week.
He missed quite a lot,
And a booster shot.
And now he feels just like a freak!

There was a man from Monaco
Who traveled all over the globe.
So many places,
And lots of faces.
Now he's resting at home—in his robe.

There was a barkeeper from Peking
Who couldn't remember a thing.
Not much of a waiter;
More a frustrater.
He forgot who ordered a drink.

There was a girl from the Bahamas
Who learned to play the maracas.
A fun rumba-shaker;
An easy music-maker.
She played for Mamas and Papas.

There was a man from Ann Arbor
Who left his fortune to a farmer.
Large sums of money
From a real dummy.
He thought the farmer was smarter.

There was a lady from Algiers
Who could not keep track of the years.
Time goes by quickly.
Forty, fifty, sixty.
The lady's age was never quite clear.

There was an old cook from Duluth
Who fell into a big pot of soup.
The soup was hot,
The cook was in shock.
And it took a long time to recoup.

There was a lady from Lake Louise
Who hung her clothes to dry in the breeze.
The air was quite calm,
The breeze was all gone.
She just waited under a tree.

There was a young worker from Maine
Who fell from the top of a crane.
He was up so high
He could touch the sky.
His language was rather profane.

There was an unhappy old-timer
Who played a song in A minor.
It was really sad,
Which made folks feel bad.
Tune in A major would be finer.

There was a young man from Bombay;
Played his whistle all night and all day.
So many fine tunes,
Too much to consume.
His wife said, “Stop, or I won’t stay.”

There was a woman named Elaine
Who got hit by a long freight train.
She did not see the sign,
And did not move in time.
So sorry, Elaine, what a shame!

There was a man from Wichita
Who woke up someplace in Utah.
A good place to ski
With mountains to see,
But he wanted a place to tee off.

There was a man named Montgomery
Who had a tiny pet monkey.
It could dance and sing
And even blow smoke rings,
But never when it was grumpy.

There was a boy from Big Bear Lake
Who owned a very large bull snake.
It ate little mice,
Which did not seem nice;
And now it has a bellyache.

There was a young man named Phil Dill
Who lived on the top of a hill.
Going down was easy,
Going up made him queasy.
He might have to move and rebuild.

There was a lady named La Rose
Who always dressed up in fine clothes.
She went to the store
And bought even more.
People now stare wherever she goes.

A man who lives across our town
Looks a bit like a circus clown.
He dresses funny
Just for the money
Which is a very small amount.

There was an old lady named Joyce
Who had an extremely loud voice.
She tried not to speak,
And then said, "Good grief!"
"Being silent is NOT my choice!"

There was a very young man named Scott
Who wanted to buy a soda pop.
Sonic tops the list.
On that, he did insist.
He wanted to see a car hop.

There is a little girl named Fran
Who is hungrier than I am.
She wants something new,
Something she can chew.
She wants to try bread and grape jam.

There was a young man named Omar
Who bought a shiny silver car.
He would not take it out.
When asked why, he'd shout:
"I don't know how to parallel park!"

There was a girl called Krazy Kat
Who always wore a funny hat.
Always on—never off,
Causing many to scoff.
Some even called her a dingbat.

There was an uptight girl named Cloud
Who would not drive a roundabout.
How to get off one?
Not very much fun!
She always chose another route.

There is a friendly boy named Dwight
Who watches the stars every night.
If the sky is clear
He'll be there to cheer!
And he calls them little skylights.

There was a lady named Sue Clark
Whose door had been carefully carved.
She left it alone
But when she got home
Surprise! The door was now a jar!

There was a young man named DJ
Who went fishing every Friday.
Fishing pole and bait
To the lake . . . and wait.
No fish today? Shop at Safeway!

There was a cook named Dominique
Who made a soup no one could eat.
Not too cold—not too hot.
Something you forgot?
Costco soups are hard to beat!

There was a dog owner named Pat
Whose dog barked a lot—and that's a fact.
Barking high and low,
Like a song you know.
Now he has a recording contract!

There was a man named Larry Lou
Who owned a cute pet kangaroo.
It hopped up so high
It got stuck in the sky.
And now it's on the late-night news!

There was a young lady named Rose
Who had an unusual nose.
The longest one in town;
Made her look like a clown.
How it got that way no one knows.

There was a young man named Larry Lile
Who had a very strange hairstyle.
Just like his brother,
He could use a cutter.
Just looking at them made you smile.

There is an old man named Spence
Who likes to sit on the fence.
He sits there all day
Just so he can say
"Hello"—and wait for compliments.

There was a young man from Frankfurt
Who rode his pet turtle to work.
It took him a week
Which was quite unique.
And now he is a former file clerk.

There was a girl named Wanda White
Who wrote a letter every night.
She ran out of stamps;
A sad circumstance.
So she delivered them on her bike.

There was a young man in our town
Who wanted to be a circus clown.
To make people laugh,
He looked like a giraffe.
But all they did was "boo" and frown.

There was a young man from Terre Haute
Who did not know how to row a boat.
When everything failed,
He put up a sail
And told everyone there to blow.

There was an older man named Doug
Who fell asleep in the bathtub.
The water was hot,
And then it was not.
His wife came in and pulled the plug.

There was a young boy from Grand Forks
Who did not know how to ride a horse.
Off went the alarms!
He broke both his arms!
He's only walking now, of course.

There is a girl named Annie Stover
Looking for a four-leaf clover.
We can see her panties
That look so fancy
Whenever she stops to bend over.

A young man who lived very near Rome
Wanted to kiss the Blarney Stone.
When he made a plan
With no money on hand,
His bank would not give him a loan.

There was a young man from Limerick
Who had a very long walking stick.
He walked ten miles a day
Wearing a green beret.
Not once did he miss or get sick.

A lady in Ireland bought some lace.
So fine, it could never be replaced.
When someone asked the cost,
She turned red and coughed.
She knew she had made a big mistake.

A lady in Ireland played the harp
Every day in the big city park.
Then the music stopped
When her G-string popped,
Ending the music in the park.

A man who works for the Club Med
Very much likes to stand on his head.
His wife said, “Take a hike,”
Sounding a bit unladylike.
And now he sleeps in a different bed.

There was a man from Delaware
Who liked to climb very steep stairs.
He didn’t care how steep;
He was a great athlete.
Then he fell and hurt his derriere.

There was a little girl named Mona
Who lived in Tucson, Arizona.
She did not like the heat
Which made her feel quite weak,
So she moved away to Tacoma.

A young man who was not ambitious
Hated washing dirty dishes.
He bought some paper plates.
Now his face radiates.
He has time to do what he wishes.

A young man could not stop sneezin'
Because the weather was freezin'.
He moved way down south
With his lovely spouse,
And the result was quite pleasin'.

There was a very old man named Wayne
Who walked every day in the rain.
One day when he fell,
He let out a yell
That you might find a little profane.

I knew a lady named Clementi.
She wore a hat wherever she wenty.
Her shoes always matched
Her beautiful hat,
And the smiles she got were aplenty.

There was a Swede in my bowling league
Who had more books than he could read.
Books in a big pile,
That blocked the long aisle
And he didn't know how to proceed.

There was a lad named Benjamin King
Who collected long pieces of string.
That made a big ball.
It stood ten feet tall.
What can he do with such a thing?

There was a man named Fernando
Who thought he could play the piano.
In fact, he could not,
And, on second thought,
He should have stayed with the banjo!

I grew up with a girl named Stella,
Who married a very tall fella.
Although he was tall,
She was not at all.
A funny couple, I can tell ya.

There was a lady named Shawnda Wright
Who could not get to sleep at night.
Asleep at the wheel,
This was a big deal
When she ran through a traffic light.

There was an old man from Nassau
Who took his dog to a fancy spa.
No longer a mutt,
But now quite deluxe.
All who saw it quickly said "aah."

There was a girl named Penny Page
Who would drink only lemonade.
Each and every day
There was no other way,
Until she drank some cold Gatorade.

There was a young man named Mike Mix
Who had a big bunch of toothpicks.
They were all quite sharp,
Like a brand new dart;
And he used them as swizzle sticks.

A young man named Bobby Bracket
Always wore a new black jacket.
He looked quite scary
In the library
With his books in a big basket.

There is a girl named Connie Class
Who only listens to bluegrass.
There's Charlie Monroe
And there's J. D. Crowe;
But her favorite is Johnny Cash.

There was a young girl named Dede
Who ate lots of fettuccine.
Ate it every day;
Too much, you might say,
And now she's not teeny-weeny.

There was a lady named Rachel
Who ate far too many bagels.
Her stomach exploded
And this note she posted:
"Sorry, I am not more graceful!"

I knew a boy whose name was Dwight
Who sang country songs day and night.
He just would not stop
And he was such a flop;
They told him to go fly a kite!

There was a little boy in our house
Who dressed up like a giant mouse.
He scared all the girls
And made them all swirl;
One even suffered a blackout!

There was a girl from Cripple Creek
Who wore only pink pants all week.
When no one noticed
She felt quite hopeless,
And the pants are now obsolete.

There was a man named Willie Witt
Who went on a very long trip.
He cut his trip short;
He was out of sorts
Because he would never leave a tip.

There was an old lady named Jackson
Who lived in a stately mansion.
No one liked her much;
She was out of touch
And she was always a-rantin'

There was a man named Gary Gear
Who bought a new car every year.
He had lots of money
To share with his honey,
But why they did this is unclear.

There was a young man named Will Parks
Who never won at playing cards.
For a change of pace
He entered sweepstakes
And won himself a steel guitar.

There was a young girl named Monique
Who climbed a mountain every week.
Then one day she fell;
Things did not go well.
Now she stays home with a book to read.

There was a young man named Don Rose
Who liked to type with just his toes.
That was quite a trick
You'll have to admit.
How he could do that, no one knows.

There was a boy named Tom Tucker
Who ate only peanut butter.
It soon became plain
That he would not change;
Every breakfast, lunch, and supper.

There is a girl named Connie Chub
Who lives next door to a nightclub.
There is lots of noise
That some say "annoys."
But that is what she really loves.

There was a girl from the Klondike
Who ate pasta morning and night.
You won't be surprised;
For the food she liked,
She always had an appetite.

There was a girl from Diamond Head
Who always wore the color red.
We all asked her why
And this was her reply:
"It's my favorite," she quickly said.

There was a lady named Adele
Who lived in a five-star hotel.
She had lots of cash
And she liked first class.
There really was no parallel.

There was a girl named Sue Walker
Who would only drink hot water.
You might find that strange,
But as she explains:
"I learned all that from my father."

There was a boy named Billy White
Who only slept two hours each night.
How could this be so?
We wanted to know.
Because his friend played the bagpipe.

I know a boy named Don Clifford
Who only talks in a whisper.
A very strange trait;
It was not innate.
He blamed it on his big sister.

I know a young boy from Green Bay
Who watches the sunset every day.
That surprises me,
Wouldn't you agree?
He said it was just his forte.

There was a boy named Tommy Wells
Who wanted to be someone else.
I asked the question;
Watched his expression.
His answer was, "I'll never tell."

There was one in my school district
Who was always pessimistic.
He really tried hard,
But in that regard,
He could not be optimistic.

I knew a girl named Kay Conway
Who went to church every Sunday.
She only missed once
In twenty-four months;
She went there to sing and to pray.

I had a friend named Gary Glenn
Who said he would not shop again.
He went with his wife,
But just to suffice.
He was afraid he'd overspend.

There was a boy named Sammy Steel
Who ate dog food with every meal.
He barked like a dog,
Which you might think odd.
Now he has even learned to "heel."

I knew a boy named Francis Ford
Who went to school on a skateboard.
He was very fast
And that is a fact.
For this, he wanted a reward.

There was a girl from the Klondike
Who did not know how to ride a bike.
You might wonder why.
This was her reply:
She didn't think it was ladylike.

There was an old airplane pilot
Who wanted to be a pirate.
He was too heavy;
So, to get ready,
He had to go on a diet.

There was a young boy from Shreveport
Who always thought he was too short.
Why did he think this?
He had one big wish;
He wanted to be good at sports.

There was a girl named Helen Hall
Who did not like being so tall.
Her friends were surprised;
They all recognized
She was quite good at basketball.

There was a girl named Connie King
Who would only write in red ink.
Her friends thought it strange
And she would not change.
She said, "Doing that helps me think."

There was a girl from Barbados
Who loved dressing in Calicos
She liked colors bright;
That made quite a sight
And she added colorful bows.

There was a little boy named Jack
Who owned more than seventeen cats.
It was not easy
To feed them cheaply,
So he fed them mostly light snacks.

There was a girl named Nancy Noone
Who would only eat with a spoon.
She lacked good manners
And had no glamour.
She had to leave the dining room.

I knew a young girl named Lorraine
Who refused to ride in a plane.
As much as we tried,
She only replied
That she wanted to ride the train.

I knew a young man named Ray Rice
Who had a headache all his life.
We all wondered why;
This was his reply:
Sorry to say, he blamed his wife.

I knew a boy named Andy Ames
Who liked to play video games.
He played day and night,
Which did not seem right.
Everyone thought he was just strange.

There was a boy from Lake Mead
Who was never able to sleep.
He tried really hard
And then he took charge;
He promised to try counting sheep.

A girl scratched up her face so much
She always had to wear make-up.
When her life got worse
She called up a nurse.
She wanted to get a check-up.

A young lady who lived in Cape Cod
Did not like tea that was too hot.
It had to be right
Or she'd get uptight,
Which everyone thought a bit odd.

I knew a boy named Danny Dud
Who would only drink out of a mug.
It's kind of funny,
To put it bluntly.
When asked about it, he just shrugged.

I knew a girl named Wanda Waite
Who watched the sunset every day.
She loved it so much
She thought it a must.
She did that until her hair turned gray.

There was a man from Ann Arbor
Who was glad to be a farmer.
He was very proud
And so was his spouse.
There was no one who worked harder.

There was a boy from Decatur
Who had a pet alligator.
To have such a pet
Caused quite a big threat,
And upset his next-door neighbor.

There was a young man named Sam Peat
Who lived in a house with no heat.
His house was quite cold
When the wind did blow,
Which left him with very cold feet.

There was a young girl named Deanna
Who would only eat bananas.
Her husband was mad
Which made her quite sad.
She took her fruit to Montana.

A rich man drove a Mercedes-Benz.
He had only a few good friends.
Others thought him a snob
And a little bit odd,
Which left him so sad in the end.

There was a young taxi driver
Who dreamed he had a pet tiger.
Then he realized
Much to his surprise,
It even growled at a rider.

There was a young girl named Gertrude
Who would only eat salty food.
She would not stop it;
Said she'd never quit.
And she had a bad attitude.

There was an old man from Cape Cod
Who did not like a noisy dog.
The dog was normal;
The man was forceful.
His friends thought that he was quite odd.

There was a baby named Tyler
Who got bitten by a spider.
As he went to sleep,
He thought "how unique"
That a spider got in my diaper.

There's a professor named Edward E.,
Taught at the big university.
He flunked his classes,
Both lads and lasses.
He is now gone, as you can see.

There was a young man named Randall
Who always wore socks with his sandals.
He did not want cold feet
As he walked down the street,
So, for us, he set this example.

There was a young boy with a mustache
Who was very good in math class.
He knew his numbers;
A real number cruncher.
Others thought he was too smart, perhaps.

There was a professor named Mose
Who always had a runny nose.
When it would not stop,
All his friends did gawk.
And said that this is not a joke!

There was a young man named Sam Tuck
Who watched football from dawn to dusk.
He never got tired
Of the time required,
And to watch? He said, "I must!"

There was an old woman named Beth
Who taught her little dog to fetch.
He brought back a stone;
She wanted a bone.
She said, "Why can't you be correct?"

Once, an old Irishman named Nate
Slept for forty-one hours straight.
He would not wake up
To get his hair cut.
As for his barber, he'll have to wait.

There was a young man named Neil
Who taught his little dog to heel.
The dog was quite smart
But right from the start,
He'd only do it for a meal!

There was an old lady named Rose
Who always had a runny nose.
Then one day it stopped
Which was quite a shock.
The reason why, nobody knows.

There was a lady from Vernal
Who wanted to be a turtle.
She was not at all fast
And always came in last,
Wearing a fancy red girdle.

An old fellow lived in a tent
And spoke in a British accent.
His speech was not clear;
Not easy to hear.
He was an unusual gent.

There is a young man in my class
Who only listens to bluegrass.
No classical for him,
Maybe one hymn.
And sometimes, he listens to brass.

There was a young boy from Foster
Who wanted to be a boxer.
He was ready to fight,
Be it day or night.
Boxing gloves were in his locker.

There was an old lady named Kate
Who would only eat pies and cakes.
She ate any flavor
From any baker.
She enjoyed every size and shape.

There was a young man named Sam Hall
Who wore red sneakers to a ball.
Everyone took notice
And turned up their noses
At the sight of such an oddball.

There was a young man born in June
Who wanted to live on the moon.
He just blew a fuse
When he heard the news;
He could not take his pet baboon.

There was an old man named Spencer
Who always wore bright suspenders.
He saved the brightest one
So he could have some fun
Whenever he went to Denver.

There was an old man from Wingate
Who ate spaghetti every day.
He liked it spicy
And not too pricey;
Served at his favorite food buffet!

There was an old miser named Leer
Who gave up reading for a year.
He would not buy a book
With cash or checkbook.
The reason for this was not clear.

There was a young registered nurse
Who did not like chocolate desserts.
She would not take a bite
Even if it was lite.
That's her, for better or for worse.

There is an artist in Peru
Who has a very strange tattoo.
It is on her arm;
It might cause alarm.
It's not something she can undo.

There was an old man in Kashmir
Who got a haircut once a year.
He would not say why;
I just asked him twice.
He said I should not interfere.

There was a handsome man named Clay
Who listened to music all day.
That's all he would do;
And that's very true.
When asked why this, he would not say.

There was a banker from Moon Bay
Who gave all his money away.
Now he was quite broke,
And that was no joke.
Now he will wait for his next payday.

There was a little man named Joe
Who got caught in a tornado.
A terrible sight
Which gave him a fright.
Everything flying to and fro.

There was a lady named Marlene
Who ate only chocolate ice cream.
You'd think she was sweet
After such a treat,
But all she wanted to do was scream.

There was a boy in my hometown
Who performed as a circus clown.
He thought he was funny.
To put it bluntly,
His show was always a letdown.

There was a girl in Monterey
Who had a dog that ran away.
She wanted him back;
She missed his loud yap.
She found him eating in a café.

There was a minister named Mork
Who always rode his bike to work.
When he had a flat,
He sat there and laughed.
So happy that he was not hurt.

There was an old person named Dee
Who did nothing but watch TV.
She watched day and night,
And thought it was all right
Until she had to pay a fee.

There was a librarian named Cook
Who never finished reading a book.
So many to choose;
They all made her snooze.
Maybe she needed one that was good.

Melanie Mert is a Girl Scout
Who has a pet snake in her house.
Her friends won't come by
And I wonder why.
Her snake would not harm even a mouse.

A young girl drove a Land Rover
And hated the roller coaster.
It went much too fast
And made her feel aghast,
Always hoping it would go slower.

There was a lady named Aster
Who climbed to the top of a ladder.
I was glad to learn
There was no concern
And that a man nearby grabbed her.

There was a dog owner named Clyde
Whose dog barked all day and all night.
It just would not stop;
That's not what it was taught.
It knew this habit was not right.

There was a young boy named Mack Grath
Who did not like to take a bath.
He hated getting wet;
In fact, he got upset
And ended up on the warpath.

There was a farmer girl named Deb
Who had a pet donkey named Jeb.
It just said "Hee-haw"
And that's about all.
I think Deb may have been misled.

There is a student from Hong Kong
Who loves to play the game Ping-Pong.
He always loses
With many excuses
Which he will be glad to prolong.

There was an older man named Norm
Who got lost in a big snowstorm.
He could not see ahead
And he was filled with dread.
He was just trying to get warm.

There is an old maid named Janine
Who dislikes daylight saving time.
She will not change her clock
Or give it a thought;
And this makes her late all the time.

There is a young man named Dan Dowd
Who always reads his books out loud.
He is never quiet
And might cause a riot
If he reads his books in a crowd.

There was a man that lived alone
Who liked to tell jokes on his phone.
He thought they were funny
But they were quite crummy
And made all of his listeners moan.

There was a pretty girl named Peach
Who liked to walk along the beach.
Always in barefoot
Which might not be good
If there is something sharp beneath.

There was an old man from Lost Acres
Who got a monthly pedicure.
His toenails grew fast
In case anyone asked.
But paying for them left him poor.

There was a young boy named Mitchell
Who would never ever eat pickles.
They always made him sick
And that was the pits,
So he ate some different vittles.

There was a man named Willie Gates
Who collected old license plates.
They hung on the wall
In a very long hall
And he counted seventy-eight.

There was a lady friend of mine
Who baked cookies at Christmastime.
They were great to eat
And tasted so sweet
That one day I ate twenty-nine.

There was a young artist named Clay
Who painted a picture a day.
Some were very bright
And some were a fright.
And some should not be on display.

There was a teenager named Reese
Who rode his bike in the Olympics.
He did not win the Gold
Which gave him quite a jolt.
He'll be back in two-hundred-eight weeks.

There was a young man named Dennis
Who would not go to the dentist.
His teeth did not hurt;
Why see an expert?
Someday he will come to his senses.

There was a gentleman from Green Bay
Who took vitamins every day.
His goal was good health
And his personal wealth.
He had a good plan, you might say.

There was a stranger in Cancun
Who lived in a dark basement room.
He did not like the light;
It gave him a fright.
He might as well live in a tomb.

There was a certain young housemaid
Who would drink gallons of Kool-Aid.
She must have been thirsty
And a bit quirky
To do this each and every day.

There was a young girl from Belair
Who was afraid of a grizzly bear.
Not a bad idea
for one named Althea;
To not be afraid would be rare.

There was a girl in a green blouse
Who moved into a brand new house.
She wanted a new place
To call her home base,
Where she could live with her new spouse.

There was a young athlete named Jules
Who jumped into a swimming pool.
At first he was hot
And then he was not.
He certainly was nobody's fool.

There was an astronaut named June
Who wanted to fly to the moon.
She had dreams about it,
She had to admit.
Just the thought of it made her swoon.

There was a carpenter named Chuck
Who hit a tree with his Ford truck.
Chuck did not get hurt;
It just ripped his shirt.
For the truck, there was no such luck!

There was a cook named Bonnie Blake
Who baked her neighbors a lemon cake.
It tasted so good,
As she knew it would.
It was the best that she could make.

There was a man from Anaheim
Who made pretzels in his spare time.
All sprinkled with salt
And done without fault.
To be sure, these pretzels were prime.

There was an astronomer named Ty
Who studied stars in the night sky.
That was his specialty,
Which he did zestfully.
He was the best and we know why.

There was a sailor from Panama
Who did not like his brother-in-law.
They did not get along,
Which really seemed wrong
As there really was no hoopla.

There was a storekeeper named Kirk
Who always took a lunch box to work.
He only liked one thing,
A baked chicken wing,
Which, at times, seemed a bit absurd.

There was a young lady named Belle
Who did not like to weigh herself.
She would not read the scale;
It might make her wail,
To see that she was not in good health.

There was a nun named Mary Mae
Who went to church every Sunday.
She never missed at all;
That was her altar call.
She was the best, is what I say.

There was a young girl named Myrtle
Who thought she saw a snapping turtle.
She even looked twice;
Maybe she looked thrice
Before she wrote in her journal.

There was a teacher named Gary
Who loved to visit the library.
He checked out a book
Without taking a look,
Which is never customary.

There was a girl named Arlene Green
Who loved to dress for Halloween.
She wanted to scare
And make people glare.
She must have made an awful scene.

There were a couple of Muscovites
Who did not like to take long flights.
They would rather not fly
And no one knows why.
They'd rather drive for days and nights.

There was a girl from Cozumel
Who liked to stay in a hotel.
She liked the service
And many splurges.
That's what you call "living quite well."

There was a teacher from Newport
Who got lost in a big airport.
He could not find his way
After looking all day.
He really needed some support.

I knew an old cuss named Peter Rush
Who drove an airport shuttle bus.
He did like his job,
But not driving in fog.
He said "That's one thing that really sucks."

There was once an old man named Don
Who had a big bell on his front lawn.
It made him feel safe
From trouble he might face
Or anything that might go wrong.

I once had a neighbor named Stu
Who was an expert at BBQ.
He knew how to cook
With or without a book.
He was a real cooking guru.

There was a young lady in the shade
Who had fun selling lemonade.
She did not sell it all,
But gave some to Paul,
Who sold it all in just one day.

There was a man from Carmel Oaks
Who drank thirty-two Diet Cokes.
He drank them all fast
To get to the last.
He said, "Never again, I hope."

There was a young woman named Tuck
Who got choked on a little peanut.
It stayed in one place
And she felt unsafe
Until it finally popped up.

There was a young boy named Buddy
Who had a tiny black puppy.
It would not stop barking,
So Buddy kept harping.
He thought that the dog was nutty.

There was a young man named Hancock
Who refused to get a flu shot.
He would not say why;
Maybe he was shy.
His mother said, “This is the last straw.”

There was a soldier in the Air Force
Who lived on a pretty golf course.
He never played the game;
His friend said, "What a shame!"
He only wants to ride a horse.

There is a girl that no one confronts,
Who burned ninety candles at once.
She might start a fire
And that would be dire.
Just the thought gives me the goose bumps.

There was a brave young man named Chip
Who took his mom on a ski trip.
She fell and hurt her head;
Then went straight to bed,
And said, "I'm glad it was not my hip."

There was an old fellow named Chuck
Who mowed his lawn before sun-up.
A crazy thing to do;
Why? No one had a clue.
What in the world is this man's hang-up?

There was a young man named John Bruce
Who drank too much pineapple juice.
It did not take long
And some thought it wrong.
Some even thought that he might puke.

There was an old man from Montclair
Who was mean as a grizzly bear.
We all wondered why,
When he lived nearby,
That he never showed that he cared.

There was a girl named Tanya Tish
Whose dog really loved to catch fish.
The dog always barked
And pulled his leash hard,
Just in order to get his wish.

There was girl named Betsy Moss
Who loved to make cranberry sauce.
She liked the way it looked
And thought it tasted good.
She laughed when all the berries popped.

There was a gentleman named Paul
Who got married in a shopping mall.
A very strange place,
But what can I say?
He was really quite an oddball.

There was a lady named Sue Hayes
Who did not celebrate birthdays.
She did not like cake;
Oh, for goodness' sake!
Why don't you just jump in the lake!

There was a man at NBC News
Whose body was covered with tattoos.
He was quite a sight;
In fact, a real fright!
He was a bit of a recluse.

There was a young woman named Gayle
Who would not quit biting her nails.
Her fingers did bleed
When there was no need.
And now, you know all the details.

There was a man from Anaheim
Who did not like daylight saving time.
He would not change his clock;
Stubborn as a rock,
But maybe he will the next time.

There was a lady from the Ozarks
Who liked to visit her state parks.
She went every week
Just to take a peek
And spend money at the snack bars.

There was a young charmer named Stu
Who always dressed in very light blue.
No other color;
They all seemed duller.
That was always his point of view.

There was a woman from Telluride
Who always watched *Saturday Night Live*.
She never would miss
And she had a wish—
To have her own show on Channel Five.

There was a young paralegal
Who was always on pins and needles.
She worked for a lawyer
That was sometimes unsure.
You might say they were unequal.

There was an old man named Bernard
Who lost his only credit card.
He did not know where;
Either here or there.
Life without it was very hard.

There was a preacher named Herman
Who wrote a very long sermon.
Some did fall asleep
And others did weep.
They were glad to hear his "Amen."

There was a very big man named Ray
Who was a parking lot valet.
He got stuck in a car
That did not go far.
He was there for a night and a day.

There was a chef named Big Bertie
Who could not carve a big turkey.
She cut her finger;
Oh, what a zinger!
And now, she's not quite so perky.

There was a brave lad named Ted Link
Who got hurt in a hockey rink.
He fell on the ice;
And that was not nice.
He said he'd rather play tiddlywinks.

Did you hear about the bellhop
Who had to wait at the barbershop?
He was in a hurry
And started to worry
That his job was on the chopping block.

There was an old man from Mount Hood
Who enjoyed cutting up firewood.
Nobody knows why
He took such delight
In working as hard as he could.

There was a young lady named Bloom
Who kept an ant farm in her room.
She thought it was fun
For someone so young;
Until the ants were on the loose.

There was a young girl named Betty Bass
Who signed up for a ballet class.
She wore a pink dress
That looked like a mess.
For this dance, she said, "I'll have to pass."

There was a young poet named Monique
Who wrote fifty poems in a week.
She got writer's cramp
Which caused her to pant.
That's one thing she will not repeat.

There was a lady named Sue Horne
Who would not drive in a snowstorm.
She did not like slick streets
Or snow turned into sleet.
She will just wait until it's warm.

There was a housewife named Coralee
Who would only drink herbal tea.
On this she was certain
There would be no reversin'
And that's the way it's going to be.

There was an old woman from Peru
Who wanted to get a tattoo.
She wanted a bird
But she thought it would hurt.
In the end, she said, "no." Wouldn't you?

There was a dentist from Vero Beach
Who got a kick out of pulling teeth.
What a strange little man,
To take such a stand.
Some thought he was a bit of a freak.

There was a young lady from Dubuque
Who loved to play the alto flute.
She played it day and night,
To everyone's delight
And she played without making a goof.

There once was a girl from Paris, France
Who went to a Friday night dance.
She did not have a date,
So she had to wait
For a dancer whose name was Lance.

There was an old man named Bryce White
Who went for a very long hike.
He was gone a long time,
And then, he did opine,
"I wish I had taken my bike."

There was a young fellow from Fort Dodge
Who liked to eat chili-cheese dogs.
He had eaten one once
In a little box lunch;
And now he can't make himself stop.

There was a young writer named Stroud
Who liked to read poems out loud.
He did not care who heard;
But he had to assert,
He really liked a hometown crowd.

There was a young man named Monroe
Who roped steers in the rodeo.
He was very brave.
The crowd shouted hurray,
As they watched this rodeo pro.

There was a person in the group
Who did not like to eat pea soup.
He did not say why;
And someone said, "Oh my!
Why not just serve him some fresh fruit?"

There was a young man named Curt
Who always rode the bus to work.
One day he missed it
Because he was sick,
Which the driver thought was absurd.

There was a young lady named Kay
Who marched in a giant parade.
She played in a band
And the music was grand,
Until her feet began to ache.

There was a young painter named Chip
Who lost his luggage on a trip.
No more painting for him;
His future looked grim.
It seemed like he lost all his zip.

There was a boy named Odin
Who would not swim in the ocean.
Afraid of the water;
Only made him holler.
“For a dollar, I will jump in.”

There was a girl in our book club
Who got caught in a terrible flood.
She was carried away,
But found the next day;
Reading a book that she really loved.

There was a fellow, quite stunning
Who wanted to go deer hunting.
He did not have a gun;
So, what was the outcome?
He bought a guitar and went strumming.

There was a young man from San Juan
Who ran in seven marathons.
He could run quite fast;
He never came in last.
For him, running was a real turn-on.

There was a young man named Bill Bates
Who won a car in the sweepstakes.
It was blue and white,
And looked very nice.
Sad to say, it was all a mistake.

There was a young lady named Gail
Who bought a Christmas tree on sale.
One branch was missing,
And I'm not kidding.
The tree really looked very frail!

There was a young fellow named Paul
Who made a snowman ten feet tall.
It got much attention;
To see its dimensions,
Just before it started to fall.

There was a young man from Notre Dame
Who never won a football game.
Goodness knows, he tried;
One win should suffice.
Here's hoping next year won't be the same.

There was a boy whose name was Brent.
He wanted to ride an elephant.
That was his passion;
He hoped it would happen.
He's still waiting for that big event.

There was a handsome man named Price
Who proposed to his girlfriend twice.
Once was not enough;
He would need some luck.
It worked! Now she will be his wife.

There once was a young boy named Mike
Who wanted to buy a new bike.
One that could go fast,
And not come in last.
Maybe he needs a motorbike.

There once was a young girl named Kay
Who cried when her cat ran away.
It was a sad time;
And at Christmastime!
But, it returned on New Year's Day

There once was a man named Ray King
Who kept a list for everything.
The list was very long;
No room for add-ons.
It won't be done until next spring.

There was an athlete from Bombay
Who played tennis every Friday.
She only missed once
In twenty-four months.
Her friends gave her a big bouquet.

There was a man from Guatemala
Who wanted to see an opera.
Carmen was his choice;
It's one he enjoys.
He heard it once in the plaza.

There was a man in the health spa
Who wanted to live in Utah.
His choice was Salt Lake,
In his favorite state.
That move would be his last hurrah.

There was a teacher named Eleanor
Who taught third grade in Baltimore.
She taught thirty years,
And loved the little dears.
Now, it's time for her to explore.

There once was a little girl named Maude
Who loved to pamper her pet dog.
The dog was very smart;
He could "steal" her heart
Whenever they went for a walk.

There was a young man named Tom Bray
Who checked his mailbox every day.
He was looking for bills;
They gave him the chills.
And sometimes he threw them away.

There was a young girl named Louise
Who loved macaroni and cheese.
Every day of the week,
She wanted it to eat.
And one day she even said "please."

There was a little boy from Oshkosh
Who loved to play in the sandbox.
It might be day or night
With or without a light,
Or any hour on the clock.

There was an old man from Whitefish
Who said he had only one wish.
No one knew what it was;
He was a stick-in-the-mud,
And just closed his mouth with a hiss.

There was a lady dressed in purple
Who bought herself a pet turtle.
It was very small,
Smaller than a baseball;
And she watched it go in a circle.

There was a cute little boy named Chris
Who always called his mother "Miss."
He never called her "Mom,"
Which she thought was wrong.
He would not, when she tried to insist.

There once was a tall boy named Blain
Who was afraid to ride on a train.
He would not get on
When his mom said "Come on."
He said, "I want to ride an airplane."

There was a strange boy from Prescott
Who spent all day in a gift shop.
He had no money
Which seemed a bit funny.
He had not given this much thought.

There was a hungry boy named Blake
Who ate a very big cheesecake.
He was not thinking,
And his fork was clinking.
He soon had a big stomachache.

There was a girl named Betty Sue
Who bought a big basket of fruit.
She really likes it fresh,
As well, you might guess.
She ate it all, with a bowl of soup.

I one time knew a boy named Curt
Who said he owned sixty-six sweatshirts.
He wore one every day.
They were all colored gray.
I guess that is what he preferred.

There was a soldier from Fort Bragg
Who got hit by a big beanbag.
He said that it hurt;
And I would concur.
It was really quite a big smack.

In our town, there was a girl named Clair
Who spent her money at the Fair.
She bought many things,
Some food and a drink.
And even something she could wear.

There was a young boy from the South
Who wanted to join the Cub Scouts.
He was not old enough;
He was out of luck.
Of this, there really was no doubt.

There was a young man named Simone
Who hated to talk on the phone.
Rather, a letter,
He thought would be better.
But to talk on the phone, he won't.

In Denver there was a plumber
Who could hardly wait for summer.
He liked warm weather;
It would be better.
How many more days, he wondered.

There was a young man from Norway
Who only shaved on Thursday.
Only one day a week,
Which seems a bit unique.
From this plan he would never stray.

There was a girl from Battle Creek
Who had trouble getting to sleep.
She went to bed early
Because she was worried.
Next time, she will try counting sheep.

There was an old man from Charleston
Who planted carrots in his garden.
He put in twenty rows
And then watched them grow.
All of this for his sweet darlin'.

There was a golfer named Dan Dunn
Who never got a hole in one.
He knew how to play
On any given day;
He just wanted to have some fun.

There was a young girl named Raylene
Who could not get enough ice cream.
She liked any flavor;
No need for a taster.
Eating ice cream for her was a dream.

There was a wife named Lorelei
Who baked a yummy fresh peach pie.
It smelled very good;
Just like a pie should.
Cooling on the shelf for her guy.

There was a hungry man named Ray
Who ate fried chicken every day.
He ate very slow
And just so you know,
This has always been his mainstay.

There was a boy we all called Dirk
Who hated to do his homework.
He simply refused,
And he never improved.
He'll never become an expert.

There was a man at Delta Airlines
Who watched the same movie nine times.
He would watch it more,
But he started to snore.
Maybe he'll try again sometime.

There was a young driver from Ames
Who did not see the stoplight change.
He caused a big crash
And suffered a gash.
His driving skills are not what he claims.

There was a young boy named Humphrey
Who wanted to buy a pet monkey.
He could hardly wait;
Today would be great.
If not, he might become grumpy.

There was a girl named Judy Jones
Who enjoyed eating tea and scones.
She was always dainty;
Quite the pretty lady.
This is one party she won't postpone.

There was a girl named Bonnie Conway
Who celebrated her own birthday.
When no one else would,
She did what she could.
For her, there was no other way.

There was a girl named Patty Piper
Who bought a new set of snow tires.
She did not like snow,
And drove very slow.
She hoped the streets would be drier.

There was an old lady named Bea
Who liked to watch late-night TV.
She turned up the sound
For "sound in the round."
Her neighbors complained angrily.

There was a student named Bill Brooks
Who lost two of his favorite books.
He looked everywhere;
Every table and chair.
He'd buy them again if he could.

There was a young girl named Kay Gray
Who smiled every hour of the day.
There's no way she could frown,
Even when she felt down.
So her smile will just have to stay.

There was a man named Bill Bloomer
Who was a fine piano tuner.
Some did not like the sound,
Heard all over town.
And they wish he had come sooner.

There was a man living in Prague
Who was always talking to his dog.
He talked to no one else;
Not a whisper or yell;
Just his dog and his monologue.

There was a young man named Drew Bruce
Who wanted to hunt for a moose.
He was gone five days,
With no moose to slay.
He went home without an excuse.

There is a young girl from Dubuque
Who is good at playing the flute.
She plays many songs
From dusk to early dawn;
As she makes her little flute toot.

There was a young man from Lamar
Who saved his money to buy a car.
Not one that was cheap,
But one he could keep;
And one that would hold his big harp.

There was a girl from Biloxi
Who liked the smell of hot coffee.
It could seem too hot;
And sometimes, it did not.
Maybe she'd like a hot toddy.

There was a little boy named Keith
Who did not like to floss his teeth.
He often just said "no,"
And made it a joke.
Things changed when his mother said "please."

There was a swimmer name Tyler
Who was known as an expert diver.
His dives were quite deep,
And he won every meet.
All of this, and he never did tire.

There was a very old man named Norm
Who went sailing in a rainstorm.
He should have stayed home,
And not gone alone.
Thank goodness, he was not a greenhorn.

There was a preacher named Ken Kline
Who never got to church on time.
There was no one to pray
During the delay.
The organist played on the chimes.

ABOUT THE AUTHOR

Ron Rich spent more than twenty years as a teacher and school administrator championing the love of reading with both students and fellow educators. As a Children's Book Specialist for Barnes & Noble, he entertained audiences of over 100 listeners each week with songs, stories, and lively readings.

In the mid-1990s, Ron also hosted the local weekly radio program *The Radio Reader*, sharing his passion for books with the broader community.

Now living in Lakewood, Colorado, Ron continues to celebrate language through reading, writing, and a lifelong devotion to the study of rhyme and wordplay. When he's not crafting playful verses, he enjoys playing the harp and spoiling his little black-and-white Havanese dog, Lucy.

For more information, visit: ronrichauthor.com

www.ingramcontent.com/pod-product-compliance
Lightning Source LLC
LaVergne TN
LVHW090528110826
845146LV00003B/1025

* 9 7 9 8 2 3 4 0 3 4 8 8 5 *